My Daddy

Written & Illustrated by Matée A. Brisbane

Copyright 2016 © by Matée A. Brisbane. No parts of this publication may be distributed, reproduced, stored in or introduced into a retrieval system, or transmitted in any form, or by any means (electronic, mechanical, photo copying, recording or otherwise) without the prior written permission of the author.

ISBN- 13:978-0692730188 (UrBane Legends V Publishing)
ISBN- 10:0692730184

How cool is your Daddy?

I love hanging out with My Daddy!
When I get tired of walking, he lets me ride up on his shoulders. It's so cool being all the way up there.
I can see EVERYTHING!

Every night, My Daddy says my bedtime prayers with me. Sometimes my bedtime comes before he gets home. Then he just calls and we say them together on the phone.

My Daddy used to do a lot of cool things with us.
He's not alive anymore.
My Uncle does cool things with us now though.
Sometimes he even takes us to visit the place where Daddy is resting.

My Daddy doesn't live with us right now, but we talk to him every day on the phone. Sometimes we talk to him on the computer and we get to see his face. That's really cool, but I can't wait to see him again for real!

My Daddy taught me how to ride my bicycle.
He looked so funny running next to me.
He kept yelling, "NO NO! Look where you're going!"
When I did look where I was going,
I was going FAST!

My Daddy is super smart! He knows a lot about a lot of things that no one else does. When he helps me with my schoolwork, he likes to pretend that he doesn't understand it until I figure it out for myself.
Sometimes, he pretends really well.

My Daddy is a great dancer!
We dance together all the time. I stand on his feet
and hold his hands. When he moves, I move too!
We turn the music up real loud, and rock out all night long!
... Well, until bedtime anyway.

I love to watch Daddy dance with Mommy!
After we go to bed, they stay up and keep dancing.
They look so nice when they dance together!
I want to dance like Mommy and Daddy when I grow up.
Me too!

Sometimes, My Daddy throws us up, ALL the way to the sky!
Then he catches us when we come back down! It's so cool!
I love it when he does that! Mommy doesn't.
I think she might like it if she tried it though!

He spins us around really fast too! Like a roller coaster! Sometimes I get a little bit sick... But it's still so much fun. He's like our very own personal amusement park!

My Daddy is the greatest cook ever!
He knows how to cook everything I like!
He can even bake too!
Cakes, pies, cookies... All sorts of delicious treats!

I want to know how to make delicious things too.
So Daddy lets me help him out when he's in the kitchen.
That way, I can learn how.

My Daddy tells the BEST stories! He reads me bedtime stories all the time, but the best stories happen when he puts the story book away! Then, he mixes up comic book superhero stories with fairytales and science fictions... You just gotta' be there!

My Daddy reads books to me and my classmates sometimes when he drops me off at school.
We all love it!
Other Mommies and Daddies read sometimes too, but I think My Daddy is the best!

My Daddy takes us camping.
We have so much fun! We sleep in a tent in the woods! We go hiking and fishing! We toast marshmallows in the campfire!

Daddy makes his special s'mores with us too!
They still have marshmallows, but he uses vanilla wafers
and white chocolate candy bars! They taste so good!
Just... WOW!

My Daddy knows how to play all kinds of sports.
He teaches us how to play them too, so we can play with him.
He tells us all the time how good we are. He says we're really good and that if we keep practicing, WE WILL be unstoppable!

My Daddy has a mechanical leg! Like a robot!
He says it gives him special powers!
I believe him too, because he's super strong and
he can run faster than all of us!

My Daddy likes to help people. That's what he does.
He always tells me how important it is to help others.
Even if they can't help you back.
Not for a reward or thanks either. Just because.
It's just the right thing to do.

My Daddy is so handsome. I like the way he looks when he and Mommy get all dressed up to go out. They look like movie stars! The other cool thing about "Mommy and Daddy's date nights", is that we get to hang out with Grandma!

My Daddy takes me out too!
We go on "Daddy Daughter dates!"
We eat at a nice restaurant and go shopping.
Sometimes we just go to the park or to a movie and we always get ice cream on the way home!

Yup! On "Daddy Daughter date day",
I get to do WHATEVER I want!
Daddy also has days that he hangs out with my brothers
and does things with them that they like to do...

I like to hang out with them on those days too!

My Daddy is nice to talk to. He always seems to know of a way to work out any problem. Even when I've done something that I probably shouldn't have done.
He stays calm and always makes me feel like we can fix it.
Not to mention, he gives the biggest, warmest, squeeziest hugs! They feel so cozy and safe.

My Daddy comes to all of my tea parties!
I like to have them when he comes home from work.
That way, he'll already be dressed appropriately.
He plays dolls and princess with me all the time too.
He tells me that I am his Princess, and that even though
I'm NOT a baby anymore, I will always be his baby.
I'm ok with that.

My Daddy plays games with me too.
He also teaches my brothers and I a lot of cool things.
He tells us that we are his Princes, and that he can't wait
to see what marvelous young men we will grow up to be.
I guess we are ALL pretty special to our Daddies!

My Daddy doesn't work in a barbershop,
but he cuts my hair all the time and he's good at it too!
He's been my barber for my whole entire life!
He gives me whatever kind of haircut I want!

My Daddy does my hair too! I always fall asleep while he's brushing it. I wake up just in time to help him pick out barrettes. I love when he rubs the oil on my head as he parts my hair and braids it. For some reason, Mommy always braids it again afterwards though.

I Love it when Granddad and Pop-Pop come to visit!
They are Mommy and Daddy's daddies.
They always tell us great stories about the things that
Mommy and Daddy did when they were our age.
But the best part about them visiting at the same time,
is that whenever one of them gives me money,
the other one always gives me more!

My Daddy is not afraid of anything!
Even when I am, he helps me to NOT be afraid anymore!
He is brave and he protects me.
He always makes sure that I'm alright. He is amazing!
He won't admit it, but I know it's true...

DADDY

dad·dy 🔊 \da·dē\ noun: a Man who is a persons father. An honorable title that should be revered and held in high esteem by both he who is known by it, as well as they who know him by it!
Synonyms: dad, father, papa, pop, pops, poppa, sire.
Example: My Daddy is a **SUPERHERO!**©

-UrBANELegendsV

www.ingramcontent.com/pod-product-compliance
Lightning Source LLC
Chambersburg PA
CBHW041538040426
42446CB00002B/145